To: _Anna_

From: _Tim_

Hot Sex Coupons

SOURCEBOOKS CASABLANCA™
An Imprint of Sourcebooks, Inc.®
Naperville, Illinois

Published by Sourcebooks, Inc.
P.O. Box 4410, Naperville, Illinois 60567-4410
(630) 961-3900
FAX: (630) 961-2168
www.sourcebooks.com

ISBN 1-4022-0299-7

Printed and bound in the United States of America
DR 10 9 8 7 6 5 4 3 2

Hot Sex

This coupon entitles you
to guess what I am thinking
and then demand that we do it.

With this coupon, let's take a fragrant bubble bath together—by candlelight.

Produce this coupon when
you want some loving on
the spur of the moment—
anytime, anywhere.

This coupon entitles you to
a peek at my diary and what it
says about you—and what we
do so well together.

With this coupon,
I'll turn you on, fully clothed,
anytime, any place.

With this coupon,
I'll show you exactly
what makes me want you.

Hot Sex

Redeem this coupon for
a long view of me lying on the bed
waiting for you to join me.

This coupon gets you a tummy rub
(and lower too).

With this coupon,
let's make love on the beach
on a summer night.

With this coupon,
I will drop everything
and let you have your way with me.

Let's do
exactly what we did the first time,
all over again.

With this coupon, you get one phone call describing what we will do tonight when I see you.

This coupon is redeemable for a sexy session with me in the sauna.

This coupon is good for
one bottle of scented oil and
a massage for your back and feet.

This coupon is good
for one order from a catalog or
website of erotic toys.

This coupon is good
for passion on our bed
until we roll off onto the floor.

With this coupon, I'll let you cover my body with whipped cream or honey, and lick it off.

This coupon entitles us to
a leisurely shower together,
where I'll wash your hair
and you can wash mine.

This coupon is redeemable for
a full day at home
doing everything in the nude.

Present this coupon and I will
count the bones in your spine,
one by one, slowly going
down, down, down.

With this coupon, I'll massage
your scalp with my fingertips
until you are relaxed and
free of inhibitions.

When you present this coupon
I will do a striptease for
your eyes only.

With this coupon, you can beg me for anything.

This coupon gets us both
new sexy underwear, and then
we can come home and model it
for each other.

Present this coupon and I will kiss you over your whole body without touching the best parts.

Present this coupon when you want to see me in those tight jeans that make you crazy.

With this coupon,
I'll make your deepest fantasy
a reality.

This coupon is good for
a nuzzling of your sexy neck.

With this coupon, I'll let you cover both our bodies with baby oil for some smooth and slippery contact.

Let's spend the weekend in a cabin where we can make love by the fireside.

With this coupon, I'll tell you
a hot fantasy tale
I have never told anyone else.

Present this coupon when you want me to undress you, slowly and lovingly.

With this coupon,
let's do it someplace new,
where we could get caught.

This coupon is good for
a deep, wet, sensuous kiss
that goes on and on and on.

Redeem this coupon
anytime, day or night,
and I'll give you whatever you like.

With this coupon, I will kiss you
as though you were a cool,
crystal lake of sweet water
and I were dying of thirst.

When you redeem this coupon,
lie down and close your eyes—
I'll make sure you don't fall asleep.

This coupon entitles you to one good morning _____!

How about a quickie?
Let's do it standing up.

This coupon entitles you to a long, luscious lovemaking session, complete with mirrors so you can see how we look together.

Present this coupon and
I will spend one hour giving
you incredible pleasure.

I've discovered some things
that feel great to me—
can I try them out on you?

This coupon entitles
you to another orgasm,
even if I'm finished.

With this coupon, I'll read you an erotic story in bed.

With this coupon, you get one phone call describing what we will do tonight when I come over.